Rhinestone Cowgirl

A Different Kind of Addiction

Rochelle Cory

Dedication

To my Lord and Savior Jesus Christ.
To my husband Kevin for <u>always</u> believing in
and encouraging me.
To my children, grandchildren, and if the Lord
tarries, great-grandchildren.

To all those un-named in Rodeo.

Acknowledgments

To all those in the wake of my life learning,
I give you credit and ask for your forgiveness
if I have ever wronged you or
if you have ever felt wronged.

To the tireless efforts of the staff at Outskirts
Press Self Publishing, I couldn't have done this
without your patience, gentle guidance and
support. God Bless you!

Foreword

What you are about to read is true. Of course, I am sure you gathered that with a label like Non-fiction being attached to this title. Still, in a world that is often prone to misrepresentation and fabrication for any number of reasons, I think it is important before reading to know the following all comes from a sincere heart. This heart experienced powerful, life-changing things at work, and as a reflection of that heart, this book was written amidst many hurts, tears, laughs, and memories, both fond and painful. Those who know the author, myself included, have not only read her story, but we have witnessed many parts alongside her.

Many come into writing with the desire to write again and again, but the will to allow these words into your hand was never motivated by profit or glory of any kind. It was done out of a deeply felt sense of obedience and making the recollection of powerful experiences available to any and all who would benefit. If more experiences follow in her life, so be it, but this testimony, even prior to publishing as printed sheets handed out to others, has helped many people from all walks of life. In a world filled with people setting out to chart their own trails, it is refreshing to know someone humbled by their experiences and open enough to share the amazing ways God can work, even today. Life can surprise us sometimes with the things it brings; we are often left with so many questions, but may we always seek the One who offers answers beyond all this. With each of us living out our own story each and every day, may Rochelle's story encourage and challenge you to seek answers for yourself.

Colby Bryant *Geeks Under Grace & colbybryant. com*

Author Foreword

Synopsis

This book started out as a two-page handout to answer the question "Are you still riding?" Then people wanted more information and it went to five pages. Then came more questions and people asked me to write a book. I thought, that's all the world needs are another book. So, I searched for some stories like mine but I didn't find one. I'm sure I just didn't search enough because the bible says in John 21:25 ASV "And there are also many other things which Jesus did, the which if they should be written every one, I suppose that even the world itself would not contain the books that should be written."

Table of Contents

CHAPTER 1

My Story

For want of a nail, the shoe was lost,
For want of a shoe, the horse was lost,
For want of a horse, the rider was lost,
For want of a rider, the message was lost,
For want of a message, the battle was lost,
For want of a war, the kingdom was lost,
For want of a nail, the world was lost.

Benjamin Franklin

As long as I can remember, I have loved horses. I would read books about them, draw endless pictures of them, and I had the strongest desire to one day own one. My father finally gave in after years of begging when I was twelve years old, and he bought me a quarter horse by the name of Gus from a neighbor. My Cajun Grandmother, Theresa, wanted me to rename him Magnifique

(Magnificent), but he just wasn't that. He was a good horse to learn on; he was an average red quarter horse with no papers. My whole family went to the new Shepler's western store in Oklahoma City to buy a saddle for him, because they were so excited for me. Dad and I shared that saddle; I never really knew why we had to share one, except that my father was a very frugal man. He was so frugal that my brother and I could only have one piece of bacon for breakfast, cut in half, so it looked like we got two. My father grew up very poor in a sharecropper shack in Louisiana. I remember him telling us one story about how he and his three siblings shared one bed; they slept crosswise on it. Almost every night, someone wet the bed and they never knew who it was. I'm sure that molded his thinking somewhat. He also told how in the wintertime they would put their additional clothing in the slats in the walls to keep the cold out.

I learned to ride with my dad's help. A few important things I remember my dad telling me about how to ride are…

First, "Don't hang on to the horn of the saddle; learn to balance without it."

Second, "Get back on, if you fall off." Interestingly enough, I never fell off, as a child; I think I was too afraid to. I remember one time some boys came up on a motorcycle while my friend LaRae and I were riding Gus together. It spooked him, and he bucked my friend off and then bolted. By the time I got him stopped, I was in front of the saddle and had only his bit in my hands to stop him.

And last, but not least, Dad would say, "Always remember, horses have the mentality of a five-year-old." What did that mean? He never said. Maybe it's because they are sweet one minute and throwing a fit the next!

My favorite thing to do while horseback riding was to take off all by myself across pastures of neighboring hay fields and ranches in Yukon, Oklahoma. The land owners would say, "Just make sure ya wire the gate back shut when yer done!" Jumping up their red dirt cliffs, and in the wintertime riding in knee-deep snow through their fields is a wonderful memory of home.

When I became interested in boys, they would call our land line telephone to talk. We didn't have cell phones then. My husband remembers my mom saying, "She probably won't be back until around dark; call back then." My parents would never let me call them back. Riding was my escape from the world: problems with kids at school, at home, or, as I got older, problems at work all melted away while I was on the back of a horse.

I started dating my husband Kevin when I was eighteen. We had been friends for a couple years before that, and occasionally, we would go horseback riding together. I remember racing each other, adrenaline rushing; it was not only the horses being out of breath, but he and I as well. I remember a beautiful paint horse named Star that Kevin rode; he could cue him to rear up like Silver, the horse on the *Lone Ranger* TV series. If you haven't seen it, you can find it online, and you will be impressed. People loved that show, where good always prevailed over evil. Kevin has always been so brave and has had that same mentality. We married when I was nineteen and he was twenty. We both had full-time jobs, and we thought we were all grown up. We bought some land in Union City, Oklahoma, and he and my father built our first home. As we got the money, we would buy supplies, and over time, they built a beautiful two-story cedar-sided home, stick by stick, as the saying goes. My husband bought us a couple horses, but when we started having children after four years of marriage, the horses became too much to care for. It was like having five kids; the horses and the boys were always getting into something. Our sons are very close in age, and since I had quit my job to care for them Kevin, worked long hours at Albertsons Grocery Store to support us. As he worked more and more and the boys saw him less and less, we decided to move closer to the store, and we sold the horses.

We became city dwellers in Bethany, Oklahoma and joined Bethany First Church of the Nazarene, where the boys started pre-school. I was raised Catholic and Kevin was raised Nazarene. I joined a Bible study group at BFC and learned so much about Jesus and the love of God.

After fifteen years, Kevin worked his way up in the company to the management position over half of the store. His father was a State Farm insurance agent at the time and Kevin dreamed of one day becoming one also. State Farm used to hire agents' kids, friends, and referrals, but with the industry becoming so complex, they offered a last-ditch effort to hire within those borders. Kevin made the cut; out of 100 applicants, only 6 positions were offered. He was offered a position as an agent in Hugo, Oklahoma. The State Farm recruiter's selling point was that he had put his sons through college as an agent. Still, we were wondering if this move was best for our family even though Kevin and I loved a rural lifestyle. We had grown so close to our friends, family, and church in Bethany; we were comfortable there.

One night, we went to our oldest son's baseball game, and while we were watching, a stranger sitting behind us asked Kevin what he did for a living. "Grocery store manager," Kevin said.

The stranger said, "You will never put those three boys through college in that position." Kevin and I looked at each other and then back at the stranger; he had vanished! We believed it was an angel visitation, so we put our house on the market.

Surprisingly, the house sold within two weeks; off we went with our three little boys to Hugo. We went from knowing almost everyone around us to knowing no one, and we had no family there for support. We looked at it as an adventure! When we got there, the newspaper reporter in town wanted to interview us about being the new agent in town. Interestingly, enough they were more interested in Kevin's short high school Bareback Bronc Rodeo career. That was our first clue where their hearts lay. Hugo is a community steeped in rodeo history. World Champion Calf Roper Ernie Taylor, World Champion Barrel Racer Jackie Jo Perrin, World Champion Bull Rider Freckles Brown, and Bull Rider Lane Frost are all from the area.

After visiting several churches, we joined First Baptist Church of Hugo and tried the public school system, but Oklahoma was starting the "No child left behind" program and that didn't sit well with us. Because, our oldest son was one of the top students in his class. Instead of encouraging him to further his education, they wanted him to help the other children learn, at his grand old of age of nine. We decided to send the boys to a small private Christian school in Goodland, Oklahoma.

We would have never been able to afford that type of education in OKC, and we viewed the move then for sure as a blessing. As part of the program, the parents either had to teach or help, so I taught art. I had no formal education. I took art all through grade school; I helped with church set designs, and our children's minister at BFC who had a graphic design degree saw talent in me. He had me paint two murals, a Noah's Ark mural and a starry sky mural in the nursery of the church. That was enough training for our little school in Goodland to accept me. As the saying goes, I learned so much more by teaching.

Goodland's education and Kevin's insurance business afforded our boys to go to college. When our oldest son Clayton first went and the other two, Austin and Dusty aka Collin were in high school, my husband started buying horses again. I wondered if Kevin thought I might have a hard time with the boy's leaving the nest? By the way, Empty Nest Syndrome isn't funny at all! Our sons were my life; we never missed a game or music recital. We loved our family dearly, and we were rarely without them. I think Kevin also took note that every time I saw a horse or a horse trailer, I just had to see if I could get a glimpse.

The first horse Kevin bought me was for Christmas; I named him Noel after my friend Marta offered the idea. He was a King Ranch quarter horse, and Kevin called him Diablo (Devil). One of our first trail rides was in January. Even though we live in southeast Oklahoma, it snows and gets icy here. Noel dumped me into the freezing waters of the Red River; he thought he saw something in the water move, and he spooked. He ran clear up to the edge of the next field, then just turned around and stared at us. It makes me laugh just thinking about it to this day. I had to keep the name Noel to help my mindset, as Diablo was more like his nature. Horse-riding came back to me like riding a bike, but now I was ready to learn all I could. Gone were the "whip and spur" days my father had taught me. I hated that technique and always thought it was cruel. I remember seeing the movie *The Horse Whisperer* many years ago and being excited to find out there really was another way.

I became a very serious rider and thoroughly loved every technique, as well as trail rides, pivot teams, and play days. I went to several clinics and tried all kinds of reins, bits, and saddles. I even bought an English saddle and tried that discipline. My favorite form of riding by far was western. I had the dream of one day getting a break and making it to the big time as a barrel racer. The adrenaline rush is unexplainable. The first time I did it, I cried from the pure speed of it. By trade, I am a full-time insurance agent and work under my husband. I believe in order to have ever accomplished that dream I would have had to quit my job to pursue it full time. I did manage to make it as far as achieving the All-Around Cowgirl title at our county play day competition on Noel. Later, I competed in trail riding, and my horse Lil Buck and I won 6th place in a Texas Trail Challenge against seventy-two horses.

Noel and I during a PRCA rodeo in 2011

I was on the pivot team/flag team for the local PRCA rodeo for ten years. That's where I got the title for this book. There is very little respect for women riders from the outside public or even the rodeo management unless they are prior PT riders. I remember one year our "manager" came up to me and said, "Why do you look so serious out there? You need to smile!" I thought,

Gee, I don't know; maybe it's because I'm trying to keep my horse under control, going in the right direction, hold my flag straight, make sure our timing is right with my partner on the other side of the arena so we will meet up at a precise moment, all the while going just shy of an all-out dead run?

We are not just there to look pretty. Rodeo contestants are just as superstitious as baseball players. As flag girls, we set the stage; if something goes wrong during our short performance, the cowboys and cowgirls consider that taboo. So, a lot rides on our shoulders. We prepare all year by riding the trails, participating in local play days and area parades. We then practice intensely for four months before the big rodeo. After all that, we get only a few minutes to show our and our horse's talent before the rodeo starts and those few seconds in between events.

Here is a little something for my pivot team sisters out there. One year, a couple of young men thought they would, to quote "help us out" and ride with us. These were guys that had broken some wild mustangs and were pretty sure of themselves. It was funny to hear them say after a spin with us, "Wow, it's a lot harder than it looks!" We also had some of the girls' husbands or boyfriends, that were ropers, sit in from time to time for an absent rider. They too were surprised how hard it is. Yes, as it is with any sport, we make it look easy. It's hard on the horses, too. They have to be athletic and, in turn, have to be put out to pasture when injuries set in. As with humans, that timing is unsure. I did have a great blessing of being recognized by my friend, PRCA Barrel Man of the Year, John Harrison. He is also known as NFR Entertainer of the Year as a trick rider. He was watching our practice one year and he said, "Watch Rochelle; she knows how to handle herself and her flag."

CHAPTER 2

First Wreck

Horses are so powerful that even manufacturers of automobiles measure the strength of their engines based on the power of a horse. Yet they are so sensitive that you can barely tap them with a spur on different parts of their body and maneuver that 1000-plus pounds in any direction almost instantaneously.

To give you a time frame of when my first significant accident happened—it was the 50th anniversary of the PRCA Rodeo in Hugo, Oklahoma. I had ridden Noel on the pivot team for several years prior, and he was getting too old from the rigors of it and developed a physical nervous condition. The horse I was now riding was a paint horse by the name of Texas. True to his breed, Texas was cantankerous, and he had developed a history of getting nervous mentally. When we'd practice, he was great, but during the performance…well, that was another story. Loud announcers, people moving around, and strange horses made him anxious, so I gave him some calming medicine as recommended by his vet, Doc Salyer, and farrier, Mouse Young.

As Texas rested, I saddled him and got dressed for the parade. When the time had passed for the meds to set in, I proceeded to mount him. Some noisy trailers were entering the parking lot. (He had been nicked on his back leg from a stock trailer the night before when we were unable to get out of the way after exiting the arena.) Texas started bucking before I could fully throw my leg over him. He bucked four times and was headed for the blacktop when I went flying off of him. I tried to break my fall with my arm, but it buckled behind me, and then I hit my head on the ground. Some passers-by sprang into action, calling for help and catching my horse. Our team organizer was a nurse and she examined me, saying I couldn't perform, and told another teammate to remove my shirt so a substitute could take my place. I was taken in an ambulance to the emergency room in Paris, Texas. I had a dislocated elbow, and it had even slightly broken through the skin.

While in the ER, I got a phone call from someone on the PRCA committee saying that I had won a year-old filly by the name of My Little Instigator; I ended up calling her Mi Li for short. I had bought only one ticket from the 4H. I thought that was a sign from the Lord saying, "Get back on!" My earthly father had passed on from a brain tumor by now. I have often looked for signs before making important decisions throughout our boys' lives, for wisdom in raising them. 1 Samuel 10:7 reads "It shall be when these signs come to you, do for yourself what the occasion requires, for God is with you."

While I was on the operating table, the doctor, overhearing my conversation with the rodeo representative, said, "You will never straighten your arm again."

I don't know what came over me, but I looked him square in the eye and said, "In Jesus' name, I will!"

Pivot riders generally use their left arm to steer the horse, while the right arm is used to carry the flag. It was my left arm that was injured. After rehab with a physical therapist (who by the way was also a believer in Jesus), my arm is straight and stronger than my dominant right arm. That same ER doctor saw me a few months later at PetSmart, and he said, "Aren't you the girl in the ER with the dislocated elbow?"

I said "Yes, I am!" He was shocked, funny enough! Still, the praise belongs to God!

I used Texas for about five years, and he started showing some signs of slowing down. I knew the next rodeo would be his last.

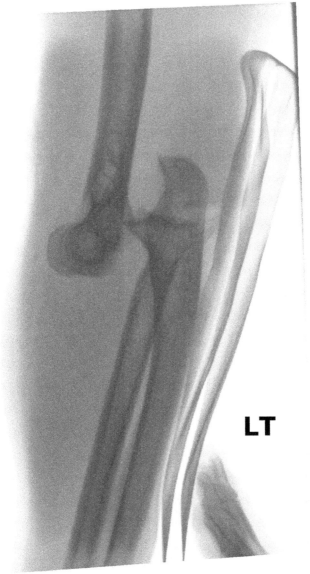

LT

Xray of left elbow

CHAPTER 3
Wreck #2

In June 2015, at the PRCA Rodeo, I was bucked off of Texas again; it was thought he had PTSD from a crash during a practice a few weeks before. At that time my partner was supposed to come from the opposite side of the arena, meet me in the middle on one end, pair up, and drive down the middle. But one of us misjudged the pairing, and we broadsided one another. I was nearly knocked off of my horse, and I would have been if my leg hadn't been pinned between the two horses. The next day, my leg was black from the knee down. The doctor said the force was like that of a car wreck. I didn't count this as a real wreck, because this type of accident was not uncommon.

During the rodeo, though, as my teammate and I were meeting up in the middle of the arena, her horse got in my horse's comfort zone. As a trainer once said, "They are an animal, not a motorcycle; they have a mind of their own!"

Texas reared twice and then bucked. The centrifugal force threw me off around in front of him and skidded me across the ground on my back. I got up and watched as the rodeo hands and some riders jumped up to help, but I shook my head and walked away, using my flag as a crutch. I was so mad! I felt I had let everyone down. I heard people in the crowd say, "Oh no, not again!" I didn't make it completely out of the arena before I had such a pain in my back that I collapsed. As the ambulance was trying to get to me; it got stuck in the mud, so my husband ran and got his four-wheel drive and drove me to the clinic, where my doctor was just closing up. Doctor Mike sent me home, saying that there was nothing they could do, because nothing was broken. The injury was to the nerves.

For several days my husband had to carry me from the bed to the bathroom and back. I was in so much pain, it was like an electrical shock went through my body every time I urinated. The shock was so strong I would scream out. My physical therapist Shane came to our home and showed Kevin how to care for me until I was well.

My husband and our sons made me sell Texas. I sold him to my trainer, BJ Schumacher. You might recognize the name if you know rodeo: he was an eight-time qualifier and Champion NFR Bull rider. He was training horses now and was glad to get Texas. His plan for him was to keep him for himself to use for hunting in Colorado. Texas used to help me pull logs on our place, so he was strong. He only had him for a few months, letting him rest a little while after the incident. One day, he took him out to warm him up. He would always have trouble with him going to the right, but I never did. I knew you had to pick up on the right rein and slightly spur him on his left side and then he would change leads. This time, though, BJ told me he took him to the right and Texas' shoulder broke. He said it sounded like a gunshot and down he went, leg just flopping. Texas had to be put down. After this happened, another horse on the team was also found to have a hurt shoulder, and as we thought back, another horse had had trouble in the past. The sharp turns and twists of the patterns are hard on them, as well as on us, the riders. We have had so many wrecks that it seemed like we couldn't get through a practice without someone or some horse getting hurt, but that's rodeo for you. Accidents for the most part are expected if you ride horses for any length of time.

I rehabbed and trained for a year, and by May of 2016, I was back on top of my game, riding horses with no back problems. I had trained my horse, Lil Buck, for the pivot team. People said we couldn't do it, but we did! I had owned Buck since he was a month old, because he was orphaned; we were very close. He trusted me, and I trusted him. I had conquered fear, although, looking back, I prayed for protection every time I rode.

My team and me, 2nd from the right on Texas.

His blaze (front white marking on his face) is in the shape of Texas. He was our son Austin's horse first. The city of Austin is the state capital of Texas, so our son thought it was fitting to name him that. I started riding Texas when Austin went to college.

My father-in-law asked, "Why are you still riding?"

I said, "Jesus rides, and He understands; that's why He gave me Mi Li."

Spiritually, I was struggling, though. I had started pulling away from God. I let situations like taking care of my family, riding horses on weekend trail rides, traveling, and disappointment in people keep me out of church. I read my Bible most days, and my husband Kevin and I listened to church sermons on the internet while we worked out in the mornings. I also did yoga, because I had noticed that something happens to your balance as you get older.

Then... I started riding in the morning and cut out those sermons. I was training my horses for our granddaughters to use one day. Hopefully that would keep them out of trouble, and I would have the peace of mind knowing exactly how their horses were trained.

To give you a time frame of the United States, this was when the 2016 Presidential Election was really ramping up between Donald Trump and Hillary Clinton. There was so much bickering and hate on the radio that I asked God while driving home after work one day, "Are you there, or are you just a bunch of hooey?" Warning! Be very careful when asking God a question, because He just might answer it!

Hooey? I had given up my foul mouth many years ago. Cursing was often heard in the home I grew up in from my father, and I adopted it wholeheartedly. But, my precious husband commented one time when we were dating, "You are too pretty to have a foul mouth." That was my inspiration, and with God's help, I changed my dictionary.

Lil Buck and I on the left with a couple of the girls from the team.

CHAPTER 4

Last Wreck

On July 16, 2016, life as I knew it changed forever.

I spent all day working with Lil Buck and Mi Li—trimming hoofs, grooming, and groundwork. It was a great day. I was training, Mi Li and Buck for the local cowboy church play day on the 17th. Mi Li had a great lineage; she's a foundation-bred quarter horse. She was smart and quick; I thought I might have another winner. I had heard that there was a huge difference between a purebred and one that is not. That was sure the case with her. She took half the time as Lil Buck to train, and he was a year older than her.

After I fully worked Buck and took him back to rest under a tree; I started working with Mi Li.

I decided to use a different bit and saddle, so I wouldn't have to swap out between horses and events on Sunday. I made sure the new equipment didn't bother her, then mounted her. We weaved in and out of the trees. I mounted and dismounted her on sawed-off trees. We maneuvered in and out of the poles my husband had set up in the field at different speeds, walking, trotting, and loping. We then started taking it easy around the barrels he had also set up. It was too hot that day to push her. I thought we would go one more time at a lope; that's when she decided she wanted to go back to the barn.

How did I know that? She turned her head away, toward the barn and pulled on the bit.

I got her attention with a word: "Hey." She had always been easy to correct, but she surprisingly reared up and then again and again and started to fall over backward. I knew what that felt like, because Kevin had a horse that did that with me before. I pushed myself off to the side of her and landed on my shoulder blades, unharmed, but she continued to rear up and fell over, landing crossways on top of me. I managed to help her roll off of me after about three attempts, but when she got up, she looked at me all wild-eyed, reared up, and stomped me. She landed one hoof on my upper leg, the other on my head. Again and again, she stomped and stomped, and then she backed up and ran forward, rolling me several times underneath her.

I thought she would never get off of me. When she finally did, I felt of my head and put my fingers inside two gashes. I tried to crawl, calling out Kevin's name, but I choked and tasted blood. I saw my ballcap within reach, so I placed it over the wounds, because the sun was beating down that day. I lay down as I watched Mi Li buck off down the tree line. I thought, *Good, Kevin will see her from where he was working and come and look for me.* I prayed, "Lord, I know you have been busy [this was right after the police were shot in Dallas and Louisiana], but I need your help, and Kevin tells me he needs me."

It seemed like it was longer than it should have been for Kevin to find me, and when he did he knelt down and lifted my cap. He then said, "Oh no, I'm scared." I truly knew it was bad then because, he is never scared nor has he ever said those words.

I said, "Honey, go get your truck, and take me to the hospital." I knew it would take awhile for an ambulance to get to me if he called one in.

On the way, I kept saying, "She stomped me, she stomped me." I was so surprised she would do such a thing. When we got there, they rushed me into the emergency room. The people in the waiting room (customers of ours) later told me they didn't even recognize me and only knew it was me because Kevin said so when he checked me in. They also told me they immediately started a prayer chain.

The doctor examined me and said he thought that I had an orbital fracture and a broken hip, so he called for x-rays and a helicopter to take me to a hospital in Dallas, Texas. As they stabilized me, Kevin called some friends to sit with me while he went home and closed up the ranch. When he got back to the hospital, the doctor was reviewing the x-rays and was so surprised there were no broken bones; thank the Lord for the prayer chain! But still, with the head injury, he was sending me on. Kevin was concerned, because we knew no one in Dallas. As they were putting me in the helicopter, he asked which hospital they were taking me to, and they said they weren't going to Dallas; they were taking me to Tulsa. That was truly a God thing for Kevin and me, because our youngest son Dusty lives there. Dusty, his fiancée Samantha, her parents, and our close friend, Brette, met me at the hospital. The doctor there decided not to take more x-rays and just observe me overnight. Kevin got there after a long two-hour drive from our home.

Dusty's friend, Corbin, came to the hospital and brought me a soft blanket and a pillow. I thought that was interesting but was thankful because the back of my head had a huge knot as well as the front. There is a verse in the Bible that says "Before they call, I will answer." I believe God told him to bring me a pillow and a blanket. Those darn hospital rooms are freezing! After a bit, Corbin said, "I can't stay, I can't stay; I'm sorry," and out the door he went. I knew I looked bad and didn't mind.

Clayton, our oldest son, flew in from Houston, Texas that night, but when he came to the door and saw me, he couldn't come in. Dusty was by my side and he went and took his hand and brought him to sit beside me. He patted me as he looked away and said, "Oh Momma, oh Momma." I hated seeing the worry on all their faces.

Brette came back the next day and said, "You will be fine and beautiful again. You have no gashes."

"What?" I put my fingers up to feel, and they were gone. I looked at Kevin, and he smiled and nodded his head yes. I was also miraculously released that day (prayer chain), and Kevin drove me home. My eyes were swelled shut, my upper leg was swollen and turning black, and I could only open my mouth wide enough to get a straw in. I had hoof prints from head to toe on my body.

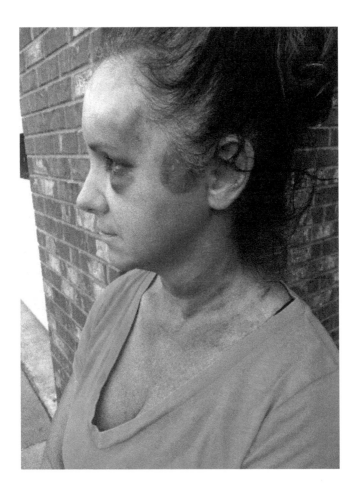

Over the next few days, I rested and did everything everyone recommended, because I wanted so badly to go to our youngest son's wedding which was only two weeks away in Cabo San Lucas. The doctor released me just in time to go, crediting it to my good health and age. I laughed, for I knew Who was healing me.

Corbin was at the wedding; he pulled me to the side and said, "I'm sorry I couldn't stay in the emergency room."

I said, "That's okay. I know I looked bad."

He said, "No, the presence of the Holy Spirit was so strong, I just couldn't stay." I was speechless. I said to our son later, "Corbin must be close to the Lord!"

He said, "No, not really."

A while later, Corbin posted on Facebook a picture of himself being baptized! Praise God, now he is!

Four weeks had passed, and I went back to work. Our staff fussed at me, but I pressed on. One morning, a customer came in to pay her bill. She said, "Aren't you Kevin's wife?"

I said, "Yes, ma'am."

She said, "I was your nurse in the ER!" She paused, and then questioned me, "And you are able to work?"

I said, "Yes, ma'am."

I was taken aback by her reaction; she was speechless for a moment. She then said, "I started a prayer chain for you when you came in."

I said, "Well, it worked!"

"There's something about the wild scenery and serenity of the Ranch and the easy gait of the horse beneath me that I find particularly relaxing." President Ronald Reagan

CHAPTER 5
He Spoke

After all this, I was wondering whether, with this being my third bad horse accident, I should get back on or stop riding entirely. Kevin and I normally go to lunch together every day, but on this particular day, he had a client ask to meet him alone. So, I went by myself, got a salad from Braum's Dairy Store, and went to the lake. As I sat out there reminiscing about the times spent there with our boys doing all the water sports, I cried and asked, "Lord, what do you want me to do? Sell everything, or get back on?"

I went back to work, and the very first call I got was from Brette. He never calls me, as he either calls my husband or our sons. He asked me, "Do you know where I am?"

I said, "No. Should I?"

He said, "I am in front of the hospital where we almost lost you. I've only had this happen to me one time before where the Lord so impressed upon me to tell what He has told me, and the Lord told me to tell you, 'You are not to get back on.'"

I was shocked and told Brette about praying at the lake; he had accompanied us many times on our lake adventures so he knew where I had been. Just as I hung up with him, our oldest son, Clayton, called. He rarely calls during the day because he is an auditor for a large oil company. I told him about what Brette had to say. He then said, "I haven't been able to sleep just thinking about you getting back on."

So, reluctantly, I found my answer and said, "Okay, Lord."

I put the horses and trailer up for sale on the internet. About a week later, Kevin asked me to go water Lil Buck. That horse came running out of the woods, so excited to see me. He came to the gate and put his head over it for me to rub. I said, "Oh, I've missed you too, Buck." As I started walking toward the trough, he started following me. I trotted, turned, and ran on foot. He mirror imaged me on the other side of the fence. I stopped at a tree and hid, and he looked on either side of it to find me. Then, he ran up to the trough. I lost it! I cried and cried, and I asked "Why, Lord? Why don't you want me to ride? I have no children at home, my grandchildren moved away, and we finally have this beautiful place to ride?"

From behind the tree, a voice came, an audible voice, the softest and kindest, most beautiful and loving man's voice said, "You have an eternity to ride."

I couldn't breathe; my first thought was, "You talked back!" I gathered my composure and took a breath but was still in shock.

After a few minutes, I quickly walked away, covering my face on the side that faced Him. The Bible mentions in Exodus 33:20 that no one has seen His face and lived. I thought, *I'm not telling anyone about this, because they will think I'm crazy.* The Lord said, "Don't tell." I heard other faint voices say *"Tell, tell, tell.* I turned slightly and said, "You knew that this was going to happen. Why did You give me that horse?"

Jesus said, "It was for that time."

I knew in my spirit what He meant, not for the time of the accident but for the time that I had owned her and the wonderful milestone experiences I had with her.

I put my hands over my ears and said, "Stop! Stop talking to me! I can't handle it." And stop He did. The wisdom was so intense for me and His answers so perfect: just the reality of it all! He was being such a loving father. He has watched me time and again get hurt, and He wasn't going to stand by and watch anymore.

We live on a small ranch with many types of animals. All other sound stopped when He spoke, as if in reverence. Just as His word says in **1 Kings 19:12**: "a still small voice." With just a few words He answered my questions... He is real, I am saved, and an extra tidbit, He did give me that horse!

Please know that I am no one special, ordinary, but in His eyes, I am His daughter, as you also are His children.

I looked up toward the house and saw my husband at the sink in the kitchen. I thought, *I can't tell him. What will he think?* I went in the house and grabbed my Bible, went to the bedroom, and looked up the verses about Jesus riding a horse, **Revelation 19:11-16:**

[11] And I saw heaven opened, and behold, a white horse, and He who sat on it is called Faithful and True, and in righteousness He judges and wages war. [12] His eyes are a flame of fire, and on His head are many

diadems; and He has a name written on Him which no one knows except Himself. ¹³ He is clothed with a robe dipped in blood, and His name is called The Word of God. ¹⁴ And the <u>armies which are in heaven</u>, clothed in fine linen, <u>white and clean</u>, were following Him on white horses. ¹⁵ From His mouth comes a sharp sword, so that with it He may strike down the nations, and He will rule them with a rod of iron; and He treads the wine press of the fierce wrath of God, the Almighty. ¹⁶ And on His robe and on His thigh, He has a name written, "KING OF KINGS, AND LORD OF LORDS."

I knew Jesus rode but never considered me riding in Heaven. So, I called and told Brette about God speaking to me and then I told Kevin; strange you may think the order I told them, but it's scary to tell your spouse an event like this for fear they may think you have gone mad. But knowing me for thirty-four years, he knew it was true.

I then called Kevin's amazing prayer warriors, Uncle Tom and Aunt Donna, our parents, then our sons. I thought I was done.

I found this fitting quote, but it had no author: "Some people may see, some people show; some people believe, others know."

When He spoke to me, I went from believing to all-out knowing He is real!

Our herd..Lil Buck, MiLi, Texas, Noel and Cochese

CHAPTER 6

My song

I thought to myself, *I'll go back to choir*. My dear friend, Trish, said after the accident, "Well, it's a good thing you have so many other talents you can use." Encouraging words are so valuable in times like this.

I have sung many solos over the years. I was blessed to sing with our sons; on one Sunday, I sang while Clayton played the piano, Austin played the drums, and Collin played the guitar in church. That is one of my cherished memories.

I heard a new song on the radio that I thought I would like to sing as a special. But I couldn't get through the song; one part sounded flat, and the words were so close to what I was going through that it made it emotionally tough.

Even though I had heard Jesus' voice tell me no, I still wanted desperately to ride. I felt like a small child whining to their father to do what they wanted to do but their father says no because he wants to protect them. The child still whines and cries, right?

I looked up the song's words and tried to sing them; then, I saw the video. To my amazement the singer was on the ground, then she was tying and untying a horse rope, and then there is a glimpse of a white horse in the woods. At the end there is a full view of the horse standing alone waiting. I was shocked, it was as if it was written for me. I cried uncontrollably.

I called everyone I mentioned before, and they were so amazed. The song is called "Thy Will" by Hillary Scott. For Ms. Scott it has a different meaning, but for me it couldn't have been more perfect. Could the chorographer of the video have seen my story in a vision? Maybe one day I'll know.

CHAPTER 7

Three tests

I got a call from a lady who saw my ad on the internet and she wanted to buy Lil Buck— figures. My favorite one, the one I trusted and if tempted enough would probably get back on. I said, "Good one, Lord."

You may think the way I talk to the Lord is brash. I was raised Catholic, and I'm not bashing them in any way, but for me to pray the rosary was monotonous. I have always felt I needed to get to the point! I talk to Him as I would a friend. Most of my prayers seem to be answered quickly; my mother has always said I had a direct line to God. Humbly, at times, I think maybe so.

To continue, I cried all four hours driving to meet the buyer halfway. She and her husband were special people; the woman wanted to know why I would sell such a good horse. I told her why but then she told me their story, and I could hardly keep it together. They had been through so much heartache. They lost their daughter in her twenties to an incurable disease, then a few years later lost their son-in-law to a different disease, leaving them to raise their grandson, who was now going off to college. They were buying the horse to spend time together. I can't explain the feeling I had. I could actually feel their pain in my heart, and I even had to turn away from her.

She said, "I'm sorry; I know you are fragile right now."

I said, "No, that's not it." Because I had been in the presence of God, it seemed, I had a deeper sense of feelings. My story touched her, but her story touched me ever so deeply. She said she would take good care of Buck and would let me know if they ever decided to sell him.

I kept feeling a prodding to tell more people, so when someone asked if I still ride, I would tell them no and why. It was interesting the reactions I received. Some people were scared of me, like I could see into their souls. Still others who had a relationship with the Lord seemed to be so encouraged. I sent out our Christmas letter and in it I told the story. I have a few on the list that aren't saved, and I thought, *Okay, I'm done telling people!*

In February, Kevin and I went with some friends of ours snow skiing in Colorado. When we had gone with them the year before, we had a morning devotional just one morning. We all said it was so amazing that we all wanted to do it every morning this time. One particular morning, my friend was playing music over the stereo from her phone, Christian music, and "Thy Will" came on. I said to my friend Marta, who has been my horse-riding part-ner for over ten years, "Have you seen the video?" She hadn't, so we YouTubed it on an iPad. Upon seeing it, she cried and hugged me so tight, a hug that felt like someone who truly loved me.

She said, "I think you are reading God wrong and that you should ride again, because you are so miserable."

I might have thought that also by the words He spoke if He hadn't told Brette what to say to me beforehand. I said, "No, I believe I have to go through a grieving time." Kind of like a step process of some sort. We both went to the bathroom to wipe our faces, and lo and behold, I got a text from Buck's new owner. It read, "I'm sorry to say but Buck isn't working out, his teeth seem to be bothering him and he's pitching." She had several other complaints but, in the end, she asked if I would consider taking him back. I shook all over. I was afraid; I knew it was a test from the devil, the Father of fear! I said, "Good one, Satan," (who is no friend of mine) and sent a text back. "Well it's about time for his teeth to be floated, I'll send a bit like the one I used," and I reminded her that he hadn't been ridden in six months, so he probably needed to go to a trainer for a month. I told her that I had been completely honest with her and to give him some time to adjust. Her very next text said, "I believe you were honest and I'm sorry, we will continue to work with him."

Wow! What a turnaround!

I have good days and bad days where I get angry about not riding. My riding friends don't talk to me much anymore. We don't have the same things in common. I feel like I've lost my identity; maybe people think I'm no longer brave? Then I happened upon this quote: "To be brave you must see the danger and feel the fear....Only then will you know what must be done to be brave."

Hell is the danger. Fear the Lord; He's closer than you think. Being brave is writing this book and telling you God still speaks audibly.

I don't want things any more. That's a strange feeling, but now I can relate to the Bible passage Psalms 34:9-10 KJV "O fear the Lord, ye his saints: for there is no want to them that fear him. The young lions do lack, and suffer hunger: but they that seek the Lord shall not want any good thing.

Riding was my escape from the world; when I got upset or stressed, I would ride. All of a sudden, I realized how much thought went into my hobby. I now have more time to think about the Lord and read His word, which is good, really good! It's comforting, and I've learned a lot. I understand about taking thoughts captive now, like His word says. But then a familiar smell will take me back, a Facebook post of a friend riding, and the team practicing for the rodeo, and I'm suddenly sad again. I have an addiction I didn't even know I had.

Test #2. Just as I got real down, I got a text from Buck's owner, the husband this time. "Call me," he said, "I have some news about Buck." I was excited, thinking it would be good news this time. I called him, and the man was angry. He said Buck had ulcers and he had to take him to the chiropractor, and he bit the trainer! I could take him back or he was going to take him to the auction or maybe even to the rendering house. I asked him what happened, because that was not how I left him? He didn't know, but he was done spending money on him, and I needed to make a decision in the next day or two. I hung up and cried, then, I prayed, "Lord, flip a switch in Buck, help him to accept them."

The next day I sent a text to the wife. "I'm sorry you have had trouble with Buck. I guess he was so attached to me. A trainer I had once said Buck was round pen sour but as soon as you trail ride him he's good as gold. Please try to sell him on the internet; he is too good of a horse for the rendering house."

She sent me a text back. "You are right, we took Buck on a trail ride after my husband called you, and he did great! I'm sorry he called you. I was mad at him when I found out. I love Buck, he's a sweet horse and I have no intention of selling him or taking him to the rendering house."

James 1:2-3 says consider it pure joy my brothers and sisters whenever you face trials of many kinds because you know that the testing of your faith produces perseverance.

Test #3. On Mother's Day, I sold my horse trailer. It was another trial. I was sad and angry again. I look at others and their hobbies and think, I don't have an addiction as bad as they do; why me? Aren't I spoiled!

Kevin and I had been working cattle all morning. I had been checking my phone but the buyer hadn't texted me that he had made it to town from Arkansas yet. I decided to call him. He said that he had lost my contact information and had been waiting all morning by the trailer for me to call. We had taken the trailer to a lot we owned for more visibility for the sale. When we got there to meet the people buying the trailer, their brother and sister-in-law were with them. I had accidentally left the trailer unlocked the day before after I cleaned it out. I started to show them the trailer when they said they had been all through it and were thrilled to purchase it.

They then started asking questions. "Why are you selling such a nice trailer?

I said, "I had an accident."

Looking at Kevin, the brother-in-law asked me, snickering, "Who told you that you can't ride anymore?"

I stared at them; I really wasn't in the mood to go into it, but I went ahead and started telling them the part of the story were God told my friend Brette to tell me <u>not</u> to get back on. The brother, sister-in-law and the wife got teary-eyed. The man just looked at me and then went to attach the trailer to his vehicle. The sister-in-law called Kevin to the side and said, "He's not saved! He needed to hear that story and he will tell others too because that's what he does." The wife said to me, "God has something better than riding for you; I will take good care of your trailer."

I'd like to think I've graduated, but I know better.

Thursday, May 18, 2017. All this week I have been doing a Bible study called "Expand your prayer life." The Lord knows I need help in this area. My focus is weak; I'm easily sidetracked. I am driving to Chandler, OK on an unexpected trip when I decide to turn off the radio, not make any calls, and pray for one hour straight. Adventurous, I know. I am reminded often when the Bible mentions in the Books of Mark and Matthew, Jesus asked his disciples "What, could you not watch with me one hour?"

At the very end of the hour of my prayer I said, "I'm finished. I can't think of another thing to pray." Immediately I get a call, and the man on the other end asks, "Have you sold that mare yet?"

No sir…really Lord? The man says, "I don't know

when I can get to Hugo to look at her, though."

I ask, "Where are you located?" He tells me Bristow, which is 35 minutes from Chandler. I say, "My husband can bring her when he comes up tomorrow." The rancher bought Mi Li, Sunday after having her all weekend. He texted me a week later and said she was just what he was looking for. People said if a horse did what she did, she would do it again, but I didn't believe that was the case with her. A friend of ours who had taken care of our place while we were gone one weekend before the accident said a black dog had gotten into our pasture and she had stomped it from fear. I think she had gotten confused after the fall and thought I was the dog because I had black on that day. I was thankful she went to a good home, because after training her for six years, I knew she had a good nature about her.

Kevin and the boys wanted to kill her, so many people asked if I had. She was saved by grace, and now I have peace about her.

You cannot easily or successfully force children into doing a sport, eventually they burn out. But, sometimes it's in the blood. That's another reason why I thought my granddaughters would want to ride. My daughter in law's mother is also a rider. An even more serious rider than me, she teaches at Utah State University in the Equine Therapy department. Her program teaches physically challenged human beings and post-traumatic stress disorder victims how to better handle their life challenges through caring for and riding horses. Horses seem to know when someone is around them with these special circumstances and are very gentle with them. Debunking the thought that horses have no compassion. I decided to donate my tack to this program. The one thing I couldn't part with was my/my father's saddle. I rode it up until the final day and it is proudly displayed in our home.

CHAPTER 8

Tricked?

Something for you to ponder....

Hobbies and interests… are they of God? What did God say we are to do in life? What does the second chapter of Titus in the Bible say about how we should live?

I used to go with my family to different pastime events. We would fuel up at the local gas station and I would think as I watched all the different vehicles that came in how wonderful it was that God had provided so much for His children to do.

But after my accident, I looked at it from a different perspective. Has Satan created a distraction so clever that it's right under our noses? Are they the lusts of this world? How much time, effort, money, and thought does it take to be a part of these activities/hobbies? I was amazed at the freedom I felt when I didn't have to think about where I had to be next, what I had to get together for the event, what was it going to cost me monetarily and possibly relationally?

Titus 2:1
But as for you, speak the things which are proper for sound doctrine: [2] that the older men be sober, reverent, temperate, sound in faith, in love, in patience; [3] the older women likewise, that they be reverent in behavior, not slanderers, not given to much wine, teachers of good things— [4] that they admonish the young women to love their husbands, to love their children, [5] to be discreet, chaste, homemakers, good, obedient to their own husbands, that the word of God may not be blasphemed.

[6] Likewise, exhort the young men to be sober-minded, [7] in all things showing yourself to be

a pattern of good works; in doctrine showing integrity, reverence, incorruptibility, ⁸ sound speech that cannot be condemned, that one who is an opponent may be ashamed, having nothing evil to say of you.

⁹ Exhort bondservants to be obedient to their own masters, to be well pleasing in all things, not answering back, ¹⁰ not pilfering, but showing all good fidelity, that they may adorn the doctrine of God our Savior in all things. ¹¹ For the grace of God that brings salvation has appeared to all men, ¹² teaching us that, denying ungodliness and <u>worldly lusts</u>, we should live soberly, righteously, and godly in the present age, ¹³ looking for the blessed hope and glorious appearing of our great God and Savior Jesus Christ, ¹⁴ who gave Himself for us, that He might redeem us from every lawless deed and purify for Himself His own special people, zealous for good works.

CHAPTER 9
His Voice

Have you ever read a letter, email, or text and could almost hear the person's voice while reading it? I have longed to hear Jesus' voice again, but I've been afraid to ask. While reading the Beatitudes one day, I had this experience and wept.

Matthew 5:3-12

³Blessed are the poor in spirit, for theirs is the kingdom of heaven.

⁴Blessed are those who mourn, for they will be comforted.

⁵Blessed are the meek, for they will inherit the earth.

⁶Blessed are those who hunger and thirst after righteousness, for they will be filled.

⁷Blessed are the merciful, for they shall be shown mercy.

⁸Blessed are the pure in heart, for they will see God.

⁹Blessed are the peacemakers, for they will be called the sons of God.

¹⁰Blessed are those who are persecuted because of righteousness, for theirs is the kingdom of heaven.

¹¹Blessed are you when people insult you, persecute you and falsely say all kinds of evil against you because of me.

¹²Rejoice and be glad, because great is your reward in heaven, for in the same way they persecuted the prophets who were before you.

I have experienced all of these, most recently verse 11. I wondered why Jesus told several people he healed not to tell anyone, now I know why. So, I tearfully accept the blessing of this story and pass it on to you.

One day, I was pondering all this and suddenly I realized I have something in common with the apostles. I would gladly take another beating anytime than deny hearing His voice, because it really happened.

I told the Lord, "I don't want to learn any more lessons." But, oh the reward of knowledge, whether I fail or pass the test!

Yes, I will ride again, in Heaven. I can't wait to see the magnificent steed that carries our Lord and Savior.

Magnifique, what an honor!